For Rachel—my beshert. Your enthusiasm, encouragement, and love keep me reaching for the stars.
—J.W.

For Christopher and my chickens
—G.V.M.


Designed by Andrew Watson and Patrick Collins



Intergalactic Afikoman
1037 NE 65th Street, #164
Seattle, WA 98115
www.IntergalacticAfikoman.com

Cover photo of Mars: Credit depositphotos
Interior background photos of Mars: Courtesy NASA / JPL-Caltech

Names: Ward, Jeff, 1960- author. | Von Meissner, Gila, illustrator.
Title: Shabbat on Mars / written by Jeff Ward ; illustrated by Gila von Meissner.
Description: First edition. | Seattle : Intergalactic Afikoman, [2025] | Audience: 007-014. | Includes bibliographical references. | Summary: From baking challah to playing Shabbat afternoon games, young scientists get to experience what Shabbat might look like after people land on the Red Planet. Full of fun, zany illustrations, this exciting and informative middle grade nonfiction book compares Shabbat on Earth with Shabbat on Mars, making predictions about a future Martian Shabbat based on the most current scientific ideas.--Publisher.
Identifiers: LCCN: 2024945964 | ISBN: 9781951365295
Subjects: LCSH: Sabbath--Juvenile literature. | Jewish cooking--Juvenile literature. | Jews--Social life and customs--Juvenile literature. | Jewish way of life--Juvenile literature. | Mars (Planet)--Juvenile literature. | CYAC: Sabbath. | Jewish cooking. | Jews--Social life and customs. | Jewish way of life. | Mars (Planet) | BISAC: JUVENILE NONFICTION / Religion / Judaism. | JUVENILE NONFICTION / Technology / Aeronautics, Astronautics & Space Science. | JUVENILE NONFICTION / Holidays & Celebrations / Other, Religious.
Classification: LCC: BM723 .W37 2025 | DDC: 296.7--dc23-

Library of Congress Control Number: 2024945964
Printed in the USA
First Edition
2 4 6 8 10 9 7 5 3 1

# SHABBAT ON MARS

Written by JEFF WARD

Illustrated by GILA VON MEISSNER

INTERGALACTIC Afikoman

SEATTLE

6

# TABLE OF CONTENTS

# WELCOME TO MARS!

Welcome to Mars! We're excited to have you here! What a journey you must have had. You're going to have an out-of-this-world Shabbat.

## HOW DO WE CELEBRATE SHABBAT ON EARTH?

From sunset on Friday until three stars appear in the sky on Saturday night, Jewish people enjoy a special day of rest called Shabbat. We celebrate this day with delicious food, fun, family, and friends. Earth is a perfect place to celebrate Shabbat!

# HOW MIGHT WE CELEBRATE SHABBAT ON MARS?

Someday, we might celebrate Shabbat on the Red Planet! Scientists and engineers have already landed robot rovers on Mars' rocky surface, and they plan to send the first astronauts to Mars soon. After that, regular families might be able to live on Mars. If some of those families are Jewish, they could celebrate Shabbat on Mars!

## How far away is Mars and how long will it take to get there?

The average distance from Earth to Mars is 140 million miles. That's the same as almost 600 trips to the Moon, or 5,600 trips around Earth! Current space probes would take about seven months to go from Earth to Mars for Shabbat—and that's just if they launch at the perfect time, which only happens around every two years.

## How will people get to Mars?

Mars is so far away that people will have to get there in spaceships launched by rockets! Maybe you'll stay in one capsule for the whole trip, or maybe you'll launch from Earth in a small capsule and join up with a larger Mars transport ship waiting in Earth's orbit. Having a little more room could be nice on that super-long seven-month journey. Engineers and scientists are also experimenting with nuclear rockets that might get us to our Mars Shabbat and back much faster.

## How will I feel different on Mars?

The first thing you'll notice during your Martian Shabbat is how light everything feels. Mars has lower gravity than Earth, so everything will weigh less than half of its Earth weight—even you! If you weigh 100 pounds on Earth, you'll only weigh 38 pounds on Mars! The other big difference is that you'll have to wear a spacesuit every time you go outside, because the Martian atmosphere doesn't have enough oxygen for you to breathe.

## Why is Mars the planet we will visit first?

Venus is close to Earth, but it's too close to the Sun for people to live there. The surface of Venus is covered with volcanoes, and the temperature can reach 900 degrees! Jupiter is farther away and it's made of gas—so there's no place to land! Mars is next to Earth, and even though it's a lot colder than our home planet, it's not too cold for us. And there's a nice rocky surface to land on. Yes, Mars is the perfect planet for our out-of-this-world Shabbat!

# GETTING READY FOR SHABBAT

*Here on Mars, getting ready for Shabbat is going to be quite a bit different!*

## HOW DO WE GET READY FOR SHABBAT ON EARTH?

*Traditionally, Shabbat is a day of rest. But believe it or not, it can take a lot of work to get ready to rest! Before Shabbat, we go to stores and shop for our favorite foods. We clean the house from top to bottom and put on special Shabbat clothes. Finally, we might set our dinner table with fancy dishes, a beautiful tablecloth, and even flowers.*

# HOW MIGHT WE GET READY FOR SHABBAT ON MARS?

On Mars, we will still need to work to get ready for Shabbat. We will want to prepare and make Shabbat a special day. But getting ready for that special day won't be the same as on Earth! Everything from cleaning our houses to shopping for our food will be different on Mars.

# What might we wear for Shabbat on Mars?

Even on Mars, it would be fun to dress up for Shabbat. You could choose to wear a precious dress or suit and tie brought all the way from Earth. Or you could wear an astronaut uniform! Astronauts wear simple, one-piece flight suits that zip or button up the front. Because some people have the tradition of wearing white for Shabbat, you could have a special white Shabbat flight suit!

## What might our Martian houses look like and how could we get them clean for Shabbat?

The first travelers to Mars will live in the spaceships that brought them from Earth, but eventually we'll want to build houses with the stuff that we find on Mars. Scientists on Earth are already experimenting with Mars houses made of dirt, ice, and even astronauts' trash! We might even use 3D printers to print houses out of Mars cement. Another idea is to live deep underground in tunnels and caves. Whatever our Mars house is made of, we're going to have to get rid of pesky Mars dust when we clean our house for Shabbat ... probably with a robot vacuum cleaner!

## Will there be grocery stores on Mars?

We probably won't have giant supermarkets and malls on Mars, because even the smallest Mars buildings will be super-expensive and challenging to build. But we will still need to get our Shabbat dinner ingredients somewhere! Each town will likely have one VERY small store that people can get to without going outside. But just like on Earth, we'll probably want to get some things delivered. Delivery robots could be the perfect solution, easily traveling between Mars towns to bring our Shabbat groceries.

## How might our Shabbat guests arrive?

If we invite Shabbat guests from Earth, it will take them months to get to our house in a rocket! It'll be a lot easier to invite our neighbors, living in homes connected to ours by tunnels, enclosed bridges, or hallways. That way they won't have to put on their space suits or get in their rovers to reach our Shabbat table. Very special guests might come from somewhere farther away on Mars. These guests could travel in pressurized rovers or open buggies. They might even arrive for Shabbat dinner in a Mars balloon or shuttle rocket.

# BAKING CHALLAH

*Baking Martian challah will present some interesting challenges!*

## HOW DO WE BAKE CHALLAH ON EARTH?

On Shabbat, we love to eat challah! Sometimes we buy challah from a store, but it can also be fun before Shabbat to bake this delicious braided bread in our very own kitchen. To make challah, we mix ingredients such as flour, water, eggs, and sometimes sugar, honey, or even chocolate chips. And before baking, we need to add yeast to make our dough rise!

# HOW MIGHT WE BAKE CHALLAH ON MARS?

*On Mars, we may need some new challah recipes, because we probably won't have all the same ingredients we use on Earth. Fortunately, if we're creative, we'll still be able to find ways to make tasty and fluffy interplanetary challah!*

## What challah ingredients might we have on Mars?

Some of the ingredients for challah, like yeast and algae, will be easy to grow on Mars. Yeast is a very simple fungus that will be used in lots of Martian foods. And algae could be turned into cooking oil for our challah. We will even be able to get salt from the Martian soil and sugar from the Martian atmosphere. That's some sweet air!

## What challah ingredients will be hard to get on Mars?

On rocky Mars, we probably won't have big fields to grow wheat for flour or farmyards to raise chickens for eggs. So flour and eggs will be expensive luxuries on Mars. They will need to be brought all the way from Earth or grown in special Martian greenhouses. While we can't make challah without flour, some people on Earth have already figured out how to make challah without eggs.

## Will our challah dough rise on Mars like it does on Earth?

Even though Martian gravity is weak, our Martian challah will rise just fine, thanks to hungry yeast. Just like on Earth, the hungry yeast fungus will eat some of the flour and produce a gas called carbon dioxide. The bubbles of carbon dioxide make the challah dough fluffy! In fact, because of Mars' thin atmosphere, we might need to adjust our recipes so that our Martian challah doesn't get too bubbly.

## How will we bake challah on Mars?

Ovens use a lot of energy to get hot, and on Mars, all of our energy will likely come from solar panels, which make electricity from the Sun. We will probably share our solar panels and our oven with our whole town! Before Shabbat, we'll take our challah dough to that community oven and get it baked. Because of Mars' low pressure and gravity, we might have to do some experiments to get our challah baked just right.

# CANDLES AND KIDDUSH

*Whichever planet we're on, we'll welcome Shabbat evening with candles, blessings, and songs.*

## HOW DO WE WELCOME SHABBAT ON EARTH?

When the sun sets on Friday, it's time for Shabbat to officially begin. Eighteen minutes before sunset, we start by lighting candles to welcome this day of rest. Parents bless their children, and we say kiddush over wine or grape juice. We wash our hands and say the blessing over the challah. Finally, we sit down and enjoy our delicious dinner and sing Shabbat songs.

# HOW MIGHT WE WELCOME SHABBAT ON MARS?

*The rituals of welcoming Shabbat on Mars will feel pretty familiar to us Earthlings, but our Martian grape juice and candles might be a little different from what we're used to.*

## Will Shabbat on Mars start at the same time as on Earth?

Shabbat officially starts at sunset on Friday, the seventh night of the week! But the Mars day—called a sol—is 40 minutes longer than an Earth day. We'll probably celebrate Shabbat every seven Sols, but we won't be sitting down for our Shabbat meal when our family back home on Earth does! Every week, we'll be starting Shabbat a little bit later than our friends on Earth. After just five weeks, our Mars Shabbat will be starting a whole day later than their Earth Shabbat!

## Might we grow grapes on Mars for our Shabbat wine?

Most people drink wine or grape juice on Shabbat. Grapes love to grow in the warm sun and rich, fertile soil of Earth. Unfortunately, Mars is cold, and the Martian dirt—called regolith—doesn't contain any helpful worms or organic material that are needed to grow grapes. Most likely, our Shabbat wine or grape juice will be artificial, or come as powder on rockets from Earth. Only on VERY special occasions might we have a bottle of precious Earth grape juice or wine.

## Will our Shabbat candles burn on Mars?

On Friday night we light the Shabbat candles, and at the end of Shabbat we light the multi-wicked *havdalah* candle. Many people enjoy watching the candle flames at the beginning and end of Shabbat. The air we breathe in our Martian homes will have plenty of oxygen, so we should be able to have our beautiful candles, but they might look a little different! Because of the lower gravity, scientists think our Mars Shabbat candles might have round flames rather than the pointed flames we see on our Earth candles.

## Will we have water on Mars for traditional handwashing?

Before saying the blessing over Shabbat challah (*ha'motzie*), many people pour water over their hands and say a special handwashing blessing (*netilat y'dayim*). Fortunately, NASA Mars landers and orbiters have found lots of water on Mars, but most of it is underground and frozen! To get the water for Shabbat, we will have to bring Martian ice to where we live and melt it! When we do wash our hands before Shabbat dinner, the weak Mars gravity will make the water flow more slowly onto our hands and splash higher when it hits the sink!

# SHABBAT DINNER

*For Shabbat dinner on Mars, we'll eat some extraterrestrial food!*

## WHAT'S FOR SHABBAT DINNER ON EARTH?

*On Earth, we relax and enjoy a special Shabbat dinner with family and friends. Some of us might enjoy roast chicken, brisket, or matzoh ball soup. Others will choose a vegetarian dish or even pizza. Often, a sweet dessert will finish off the Shabbat meal!*

# WHAT MIGHT WE EAT FOR SHABBAT DINNER ON MARS?

*When we sit down to our Shabbat dinner on Mars, we won't have as many different foods as we do at home. Everything will have to be sent on rockets from Earth or grown on special Martian farms. Getting our favorite Shabbat treats on Mars will be challenging!*

## Why won't we take all our favorite Shabbat foods to Mars?

When we go into a grocery store on Earth, we have thousands and thousands of choices. In a big store, there are whole aisles of different fruits, meats, fish, drinks, and everything else we might want to eat on Shabbat. Why can't we just have all the same choices on Mars? Because building rockets and launching them away from Earth's gravity is super-expensive. Today it would cost you $500 just to launch a single challah into space. Imagine what it would cost to get your entire Shabbat meal!

## Why won't we be able to grow our Shabbat foods on Mars?

Can't we just grow everything we want for Shabbat dinner on Mars? Martian farming is going to be hard. Earth plants need sunlight, warmth, fertile soil, and water. On Mars, the sun is weaker, the weather's always cold, the water is frozen, and the soil is sterile, so our Shabbat foods on Mars will likely be grown in greenhouses where we can provide extra light, specially prepared soil, and carefully melted water. One thing that IS easy to grow on Mars is algae! Picture your Martian Shabbat dinner—seaweed salad, anyone?

## Will we have Shabbat brisket or chicken on Mars?

Many people like a Shabbat dinner where they eat delicious brisket or roast chicken. But farm animals need a lot of space to live in and plants to eat. Scientists think the main animals we'll eat on Mars will probably be...bugs! Fortunately for Jews who keep kosher, there are at least three types of kosher bugs we could raise on Mars. Instead of digging into an unappetizing pile of grasshoppers for Shabbat, scientists are planning to use 3D printers to turn insects and algae into delicious-tasting "brisket" and "chicken," a lot like the plant-based meat many people already buy on Earth.

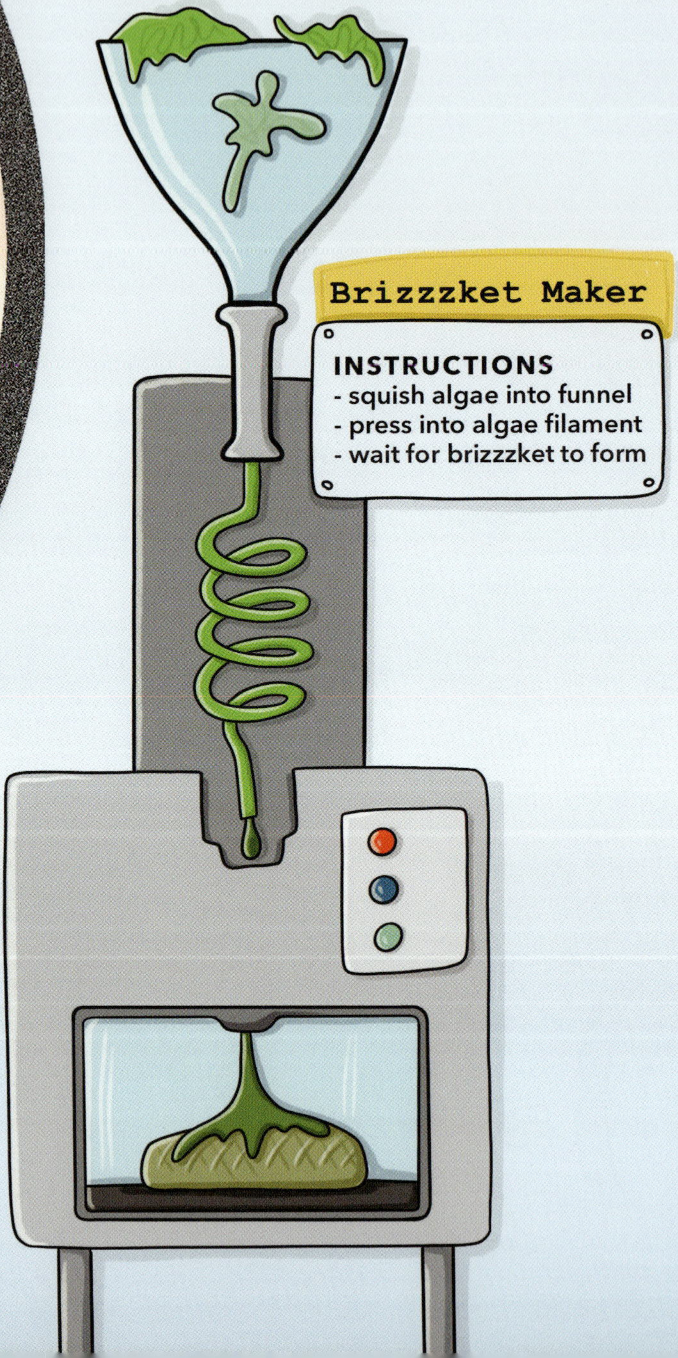

## So what about chicken soup with matzoh balls?

If you want Bubbe's chicken soup for Shabbat, we might take some of that 3D-printed "chicken," add veggies grown in our Martian greenhouse, and cook her delicious recipe. For the matzoh balls, we'll use flour brought by rocket from Earth, or maybe some precious wheat grown in our Martian greenhouses. Add that to cooking oil made from algae and baking soda from Earth and you'll make some fluffy matzoh balls. Even if it's a little different from Earth, Bubbe's Martian chicken soup should taste delicious here too! *B'tayavon!*

# MARTIAN SYNAGOGUES

On Friday night and Saturday morning, we could gather to pray at Martian synagogues.

## WHERE DO JEWS PRAY ON EARTH?

On Earth, many Jews go to synagogues on Shabbat. We put on our special Shabbat clothes and then make our way to synagogue. Inside the synagogue building, we sing and pray, listen to stories from the Torah scroll, and then enjoy a community lunch with our family and friends.

# WHERE MIGHT JEWS PRAY ON MARS?

*Designing our Martian synagogues and other buildings won't be easy. It's so expensive to launch heavy bricks and steel from Earth, we will have to use what we can find on Mars. And we will have to make our synagogue totally airtight, to keep our oxygen in and the pesky Martian dust out.*

## What might synagogues look like on Mars?

On Earth, many synagogues are beautiful buildings, with large rooms called sanctuaries, where Jewish people meet for Shabbat and holiday prayer services. On Mars, we might build our synagogue in a tunnel, a cave, an inflatable bubble on the Martian surface, or even using bricks of ice or glass! That would give us a great view of the Martian landscape on Shabbat morning. Also, scientists are experimenting with growing furniture using fungi and bacteria! Can you imagine...ark, pews, *bimah*...all made of mushrooms?

## What direction will we pray on Mars?

Some people have a custom of facing the direction of Jerusalem when they say their Shabbat prayers in synagogue. But which way is Jerusalem when you're on Mars? Jerusalem is on Earth, and Earth could be anywhere in the sky as it orbits the Sun. Maybe our Martian synagogue will have a special moving pointer set to show the current direction to Earth, so that we can face Jerusalem when we pray on Shabbat.

## How might we lift the Torah on Mars?

Every Shabbat, after the Torah is read, someone lifts the heavy scroll and spreads it out for everyone to see. This is called *hagbah*. On Mars, where gravity is less than half of Earth's, the Torah will be lighter, and you won't have to be super-strong to lift it for *hagbah*. But you can still only spread it as wide as your arms can reach!

## When might I have my bar, bat, or b' mitzvah on Mars?

It is traditional for Jewish kids to have a special celebration in synagogue when they turn twelve or thirteen years old. But watch out! If you wait for thirteen Martian years, you'll be twenty-four Earth years old! That's because Mars takes 687 days to go around the Sun, but Earth only takes 365. If you want to be a teen and not an adult when you celebrate, you'd better just count the Earth years to decide when to schedule your big Shabbat!

# SHABBAT GAMES

Saturday afternoon will be the perfect time for Shabbat fun and games—Martian style!

## WHAT SHABBAT GAMES DO KIDS PLAY ON EARTH?

On Earth, Shabbat afternoon is a time when kids play while parents rest. On a cold or rainy day, kids might stay inside playing board games. If it's nice out, they could take a Shabbat walk or play basketball, football, or even a fierce game of gaga.

# WHAT MIGHT SHABBAT AFTERNOON BE LIKE ON MARS?

On Mars, kids will still love playing games on Shabbat afternoon, and their parents will need a Shabbat nap! As well as familiar Earth games with Martian twists, you might even invent some new Martian sports.

## Why will I feel like a superstar athlete on Mars? The weak gravity on Mars is going to help us jump higher, throw farther, and maybe even run faster on Shabbat afternoon. Might we invent new Shabbat sports for Mars?

Mars' atmosphere and gravity will change every sport we bring from Earth! Whether we're throwing a frisbee or running a race, gravity creates the challenges, the thrills, and the world records. On Mars, we might invent some new Martian sports to play on Shabbat afternoon—or at least change some rules! Basketball hoops might be higher, football fields larger, and running races longer. Then we might want rules to stop players from jumping right out of the stadium.

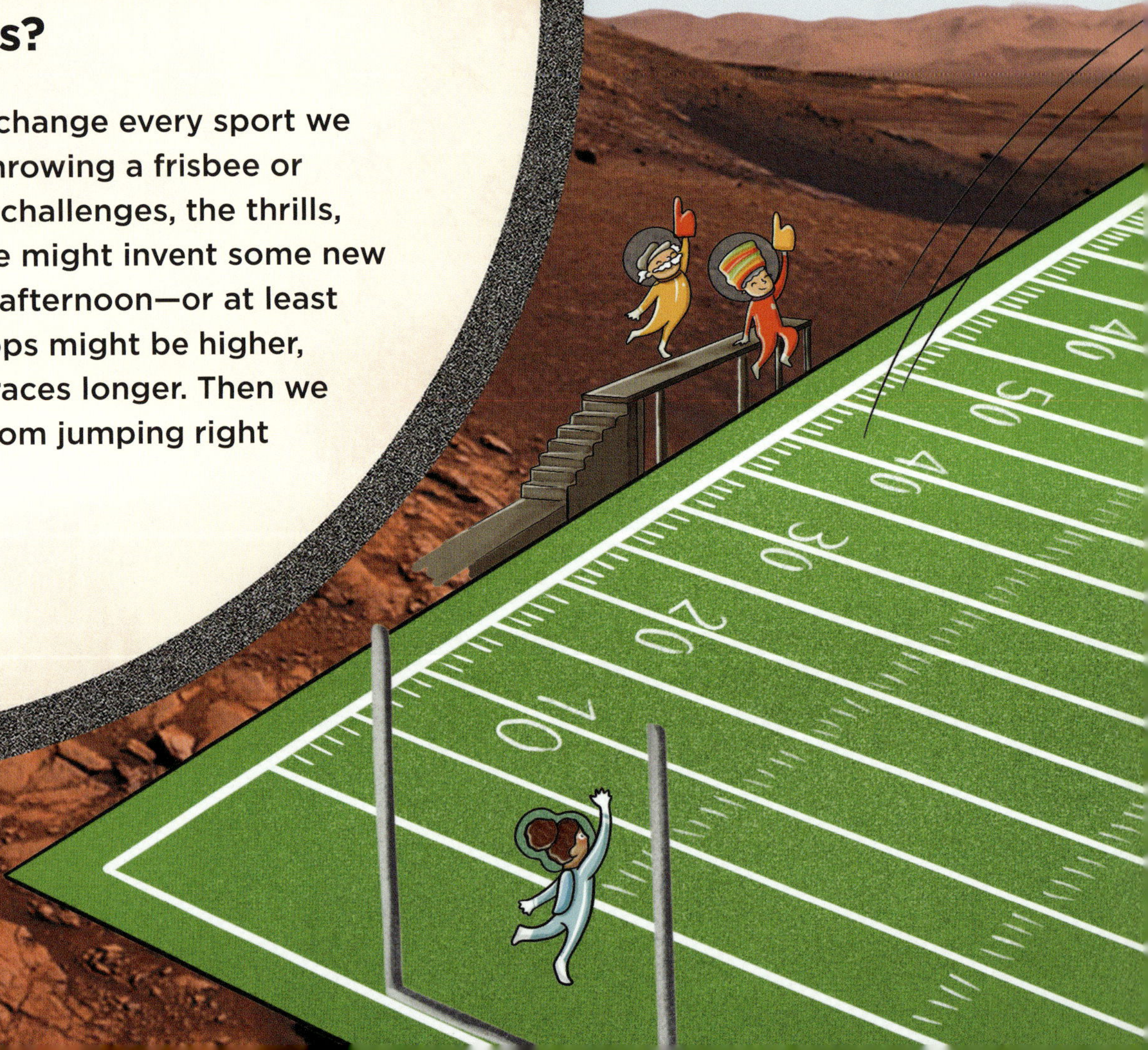

## How might we play Martian gaga?

On Earth, the gaga pit can be inside or outside, but on Mars we'll probably have to play inside because our space suits would make it too hard to jump around. The lower gravity on Mars will let you jump away from the gaga ball faster than on Earth, but watch out, because the ball will bounce higher and farther too! We're going to need taller walls on our gaga pit or we're going to lose that ball!

## What's Gaga?

Gaga is kind of like a game of tag played with a bouncy ball inside an enclosed space. All the players jump into a gaga pit and knock the ball around with their hands. If the ball touches someone below the knee, they're out!

## How might we take a Shabbat walk?

Going outside for our Shabbat walk on Mars will be a really big deal! The atmosphere on Mars is mostly carbon dioxide ($CO_2$) that we can't breathe, and the air pressure is as low as on top of Mount Everest! To take our Shabbat walk outside, we'll have to put on a special suit and bring along tanks of air—like an underwater SCUBA diver on Earth. Lucky for us, our helmets will have big glass windows so that we can enjoy the view as we stroll around the dusty, rocky surface of Mars.

MOON
JUPITER
EARTH

# THREE STARS IN THE SKY

As the distant sun sets and stars come out, it's time to say goodbye to Shabbat on Mars.

## HOW DO WE SAY GOODBYE TO SHABBAT ON EARTH?

On Earth, Saturday evening is the end of Shabbat. When it's dark enough to see three stars in the sky, we say farewell to our day of rest. We sing the havdalah prayer over a cup of wine, sweet-smelling spices, and a braided candle.

# HOW MIGHT WE SAY GOODBYE TO SHABBAT ON MARS?

*On Mars, three stars on Saturday evening will still mark the end of Shabbat, even if the day was a little bit longer and the setting sun is a little bit smaller. At the end of our special day, we will gather with our family and friends to sing havdalah and bring in a sweet new week.*

## How long is Shabbat on Mars?

Jewish tradition says that Shabbat begins at sundown on Friday and ends when you can see three stars on Saturday night. Since the Sol—the Martian day—lasts 24 hours and 37 minutes, you have at least an extra half hour of Shabbat! There might even be more, because dust floating in the Martian atmosphere will make the twilight last longer and three stars take longer to appear. Consult your Martian rabbi!

## What does sunset look like on Mars?

Shabbat on Mars will end with a surprise. Instead of the sky being blue and the sunset being orange like it is back home on Earth, you'll see the reverse. Mineral dust in the Martian atmosphere makes the daytime sky on Mars yellowish-orange—like butterscotch. At sunset, the area right around the Sun will be blue!

## What will you see in the night sky from Mars?

When you're looking up on Saturday evening to find three stars marking the end of Shabbat, **make sure not to count** *the Earth and the Moon, which you* **might** *see even without a telescope!* Remember to wave! You can also look for familiar constellations, because Mars and Earth are still pretty close together compared to all those stars. Constellations will keep their familiar shapes, and you should see the same Orion's Belt and Big Dipper that you see on Earth.

Shavua tov,
Earth!

## Can we call our distant family and friends to share about our exciting Shabbat?

If you want to call your friends and family back on Earth after Shabbat, remember that Shabbat may be long over for them. It could be a school day, or even the middle of the night! Also, it can take as long as 24 minutes for telephone signals to go all the way from Mars to Earth. When you say *Shavuah tov* ("Good Week"), your friend on Earth won't hear you for 24 minutes. And when your friend replies "How was your Shabbat?" you'll hear them 48 minutes after you made your call. Maybe it's easier to text or send an email to share stories of your Shabbat on Mars!

MOON
JUPITER
EARTH
Shavua tov, Earth!

## WHO IS OUR MARTIAN TOUR GUIDE?

Curiosity, the popular and famous Mars rover, has been your faithful and friendly guide to Shabbat on Mars. Launched on a NASA rocket in 2011 and gently lowered onto the surface by a sky crane in 2012, Curiosity has been exploring ever since, sending cool scientific data and photos back to Earth. The real Curiosity looks a bit different from the simple drawings in this book—she's the size of a small car and packs a nuclear power plant and ten scientific instruments! So far, Curiosity has celebrated more than 12 birthdays on Mars and traveled more than 22 miles in search of scientific discovery. She also loves to send special birthday messages on social media!

## A NOTE FROM JEFF – YOUR ROCKET SCIENTIST AUTHOR!

When my wife Rabbi Rachel Kobrin asked me to join her friend Rabbi Laurie Matzkin as guest speaker for a "PJ Library Space Shabbat Story Time," little did I know that I would meet the editor who would invite me to write this wonderful book, which combines my twin passions: space exploration and Jewish practice. I guess that's what happens when a Jewish aerospace engineer marries a Conservative rabbi.

To figure out what Shabbat on Mars might really be like, I read a lot of articles about the plans and experiments of expert space engineers, then imagined how the unique challenges of the Red Planet might change our Shabbat rituals. I was surprised to find that things like games and synagogue services could stay the same, while other things—especially our favorite foods—will be very different on Mars.

I hope my words and Gila's enchanting drawings inspire you with the excitement, curiosity, and joy that I get from satellites, rockets, planets, stars, candles, kiddush, challah, singing, and Shabbat naps. Next Friday night, I invite you to take a moment to remember that Jews have celebrated Shabbat with the same rituals for thousands of years in different kinds of homes all around the Earth. Then, twenty-six hours later, when you're looking for three stars to begin the new week, I invite you to gaze up into the night sky and imagine future generations of Jews taking the gift of Shabbat—our weekly pause for love, community, and regeneration—to Mars and even the stars!

# WHAT DOES JEWISH LOOK LIKE... ON MARS?

Just like there are many different ways to look and be Jewish on Earth, there will be many different ways to look and be Jewish on Mars. Jews on Mars will have all kinds of different hair colors, eye colors, and skin colors. Some families might have a mom, a dad, and two kids. Other families might have a Bubbe living with them. And another family might have two dads or two moms and their little girl.

In addition to all this wonderful Jewish variety you can see in our Martian illustrations, there will also be Jews with different traditions on Mars. Some will follow Jewish traditions strictly and others might not follow them at all. Our first Martian settlers represent both Ashkenazic and Sephardic Jewish heritages.

When people first think of being Jewish, they often think of Ashkenazic (Eastern European) foods and traditions. Matzoh Balls in Chicken Soup, Brisket, and Yiddish. But among our first Martian Jewish settlers, we also have a Sephardic Jewish family.

Instead of Yiddish, our Sephardic family sprinkles their speech with Ladino (Judeo-Spanish). Instead of gefilte fish, their Shabbat food specialties include pishcado con tomate (salmon in tomato sauce). Their grandparents (who have fun playing leap frog on Mars) are called Nona and Papu, and when Papu makes the kiddush blessing, his young grandchild follows the Sephardic tradition of pouring a small cup of water into the wine. Even Sephardic synagogue traditions are different than Ashkenazic Jews. A child may wear a tallit for prayer services when he is still very young (rather than waiting for his Bar Mitzvah or his wedding).

Wow! It is exciting to see how many different ways there are to look (and be) Jewish on Mars! How many different kinds of Jewish families and traditions can you spot during *Shabbat on Mars*?

## FURTHER READING

Kids who enjoyed *Shabbat on Mars* might also try

O'Brien, P. (2009). *You are the first kid on Mars*. Penguin.

Aldrin, B. (2015). *Welcome to Mars: Making a home on the Red Planet*. National Geographic Kids.

Adults looking for detailed discussions of Jewish law (*halachah*) in space can start with the original discussion by Rabbi Azriel Rosenfeld, and work from there:

Rosenfeld, A. (1964). THE SABBATH IN THE SPACE AGE. *Tradition: A Journal of Orthodox Jewish Thought*, *7*(1), 27–33. http://www.jstor.org/stable/23255979

## BIBLIOGRAPHY


Allain, R. (2015, October 28). How would football work if you played it on Mars? *WIRED*. https://www.wired.com/2015/10/physics-how-would-you-play-football-on-mars/

Crane, L. (2024, August 14). We keep finding water on Mars – here are all the places it might be. *New Scientist*. https://www.newscientist.com/article/2443738-we-keep-finding-water-on-mars-here-are-all-the-places-it-might-be/

*Earth from Mars - NASA Science*. (n.d.). https://science.nasa.gov/resource/earth-from-mars/

Fraser, E. D. G., & Newman, L. (2022). *Dinner on Mars: The technologies that will feed the Red Planet and transform agriculture on Earth*. ECW Press.

Hrala, J. (2016, December 30). *NASA just released its incredibly cool concept for houses on Mars : ScienceAlert*. ScienceAlert. https://www.sciencealert.com/nasa-might-build-ice-homes-on-mars

*Mars: Facts - NASA Science*. (n.d.). https://science.nasa.gov/mars/facts/

*NASA CO2 Conversion Challenge*. (n.d.). https://www.co2conversionchallenge.org/

OMSI. (2022, December 15). *Can we bake a cake on Mars?* [Video]. YouTube. https://www.youtube.com/watch?v=AiUM4ebwaVw

Roach, M. (2010). *Packing for Mars: The curious science of life in the void.* W. W. Norton & Company.

Roberts, K. (2022, August 9). *Extraterrestrial Cement.* UDaily. https://www.udel.edu/udaily/2022/august/extraterrestrial-cement-building-materials-moon-mars-space-construction/

Rosenfeld, A. (1964). THE SABBATH IN THE SPACE AGE. *Tradition: A Journal of Orthodox Jewish Thought*, *7*(1), 27–33. http://www.jstor.org/stable/23255979

Sanders, R. (2022, April 28). *Solar beats nuclear at many potential settlement sites on Mars - Berkeley News.* Berkeley News. https://news.berkeley.edu/2022/04/27/solar-beats-nuclear-at-many-potential-settlement-sites-on-mars/

Shurpin, Y. Chabad.org. (2020, January 26). *Why are grasshoppers (locusts) kosher for some Jews?* Chabad. https://www.chabad.org/library/article_cdo/aid/4624319/jewish/Why-Are-Grasshoppers-Locusts-Kosher-for-Some-Jews.htm

Sloan, M. (2023, May 18). *Great balls of fire: How flames behave in space.* Astronomy Magazine. https://www.astronomy.com/science/great-balls-of-fire-how-flames-behave-in-space/

**JEFF WARD** became fascinated with space as a child, peering at the stars and planets through homemade telescopes built by his dad and their astronomer friends. His favorite things on TV were the NASA Saturn V launches and the first Moon landing, and he painted a target in front of his house when the SkyLab space station was falling to Earth. (*It missed*.) Inspired by the wonders of space, he built his first satellite ground station as a teenager, went on to become an engineer, and enjoyed a career building satellites, rockets, and space capsules in England and America. When he's not thinking about *Shabbat on Mars*, he's walking Luna, the family goldendoodle, helping out at his wife's synagogue, and writing poetry or science fiction. He lives with his spouse, and is a proud dad and stepdad to three incredible kids.

**GILA VON MEISSNER** is an illustrator from North Germany. She lives with her Israeli cat Boi and energetic dog Mokka in a tiny house in the boondocks. She loves jasmine tea, country music, and Tel Aviv.